Joseph Idicheria (aka Jo Humble) was born in AbuDhabi, UAE, brought up in Trivandrum, Kerala, India and currently working in Mumbai, Maharashtra, India. Born in August as a Leo with it's traits in the dreams, while in real, a silent person whose written words on paper are louder than those spoken.
This is his first ever collection of poems being published.

English Language
Stock in Boiling Pot
(Poems)
by
Joseph Idicheria
◆

Published in August 2024
by Kairali Books Private Limited
Thalikkavu Road, Kannur.
Ph : 0497-2761200
E-Mail : kairalibooksknr@gmail.com
◆

Cover Design
Prasanth Mangad
◆

41/24-25/Sl.No.1608/100/NS.18.6
ISBN 978-93-5973-525-2

STOCK IN BOILING POT

Joseph Idicheria

Kairali Books

CONTENTS

Beginning and Birth

Wind blew, blew with all its might,
Rain poured, poured from a great height,
Fire burned, burned everything in its sight,
Earth shook, shook and took everyone with it,
But I stood tall, stronger than ever,
Believed and proved, I can't be killed, never.

History grew with stories of war to be told,
Ancestors died hoping for peace to behold,
Mothers cried, for a living, their wombs were sold,
Men brew spirits, to drink their pain in numbing cold,
But I stood tall, stronger than ever,
Watched and learned, humans won't change, never.

We were born to rule, every soul thought,
Violence birthed, into this world insanity was brought,
Amidst all these, some tied each with love in a knot,
Trusting to conquer anger, humanity they sought,
But I, stood tall, stronger than ever,
Praying, an angel they see in each other.

I'm from beginning, waiting to be found without cease,
Born from every human, through difficulty and ease,
What I ask , gift yourselves, part of me with peace,
And witness the world change to a better place,
I'm known to this world, behold… I'm Silence.

○

For the unborn

Oh! Cry o' little one, cry until fed,
Bent knees, bowed heads, world feeds on pleads,
They just stood up, war killed, even the dead,
Wanting for peace, urging you to plead,
Conspire to rule, every secret they spread,
Two beliefs, one love, only see you bleed,
Chromosome or hormones, they give no heed,
Gave forth a view, you born out of wicked deed,
For acceptance gather like ones, think you mislead,
Dread the truth, confine you in a cult or creed.

Oh! Hush o' little one, silence your breath,
Secret is to stay alive, evade the planned death,
Hide in dawn, hunt in dark, with anything from hearth,
Slide out and from under, their coffin and wreath.

○

Mom... our Angel

The greatest blessing God has bestowed on us,
our Dear Mom,
Another word or example for unconditional love,
our dear Mom,
The one anyone can count on at any hour of the day,
our dear Mom,
Always striving to make others happy even when she's sad,
our dear Mom,
Infinite gratitude to the Almighty for giving you to us,
our dear Mom,
Always loved us the way we're when others didn't, you're
our dear Angel,
Worries about us, covers us with unending care,
our praying Angel,
Fed us with the most tastiest food we've ever had,
our blessed Angel,
Went through difficulties, brought us up,
our strongest Angel,
Thank you for Everything you've done for us,
Our Mom, Our Angel.

○

Mother…. Two-gether

They had anticipation, to witness the new beginning,
Shelter and food inside the dark womb, always smiling,
Still there was peace, even when world around was shaking,
Growing inside, their own image, hopes of a life fulfilling,
Both together make everything better, mothers kept wishing.

It was beautiful, their first cry, first dance and breath,
One was taught, other by itself, to share during growth,
Destiny played, one hurt the other with all strength,
Either burned or buried, destiny joined them together in death,
Raised by two great mothers – one human other Earth

○

Leap of Love

Never was fond of watching sunrise,
Till I viewed from between your curls,
Met first in my city, during your friend's wedding,
More gorgeous than the bride, my eyes stuck,
Got to talk through a common friend in a bar,
That night we found ourselves on a long ride,
Coffee from Starbucks, Burgers from McD,
Halfway, you slept, with a shocking blind trust,
Next day on a hill, got to see that sunrise,
Roamed around, eating, singing and dancing,
That evening, had to drop you at your hotel,
 One day later, you were on a plane to your city,
Two days gone, I found myself outside your home,
With a banner saying, " You're my everything".

○

One who loved a Goddess – PART 1

How do you decipher one is wise?
By all the worldly knowledge sought?
Or the amount of life lessons learned?
If latter, one wise man preached,
About previous birth and karmic bond,
All those we meet are not strangers,
But related to us in our previous,
If that's true, what was he before?
Or the relation he had with her?
None knew, one thing now he knew,
Plummet, did he, in love with a goddess.

Oh! I'm a mere human, how it ensue,
From the sight of a halo, I did pursue,
Where, lust abundant, heart desolate,
She came to be, her love inordinate.

Inept, I, may be her creation, a mortal,
Or created for her, a blessing that's natal,
Credence, till this day, the play of destiny,
Reality, she chose for herself till infinity.

○

One who loved a goddess – PART 2

She was there, for sure she was there,
Did she ever showed her absence, never,
My century old memory, can't remember,
Outright forage of time, a slight ember,
None found, for sure she was there,
Unseeing was I, for sure she was there,
Proof you all demand like a non-believer,
All the times I smiled, for she was there.

Did she ever showed her absence, never,
Unlit time occlude, those she dissever,
To be my light… nothing lasts forever,
An antique accord, from her maker,
A fleeting role, to be my life mentor,
Lessons..to be gone, after she render,
Maker had plans, but time had love in favor,
And it fooled, it did blind the seer,
Goddess loved a human so mere,
Her pure heart, from a promise won't defer,
Which I dread, and that finale I fear,
Her love for me and mine for her,
Strong… hope, the destiny it veer.

O

Sung by seasons

As I remember back, all began with joy,
Elegant, vibrant deeds and scented feelings,
Shared our story, by many, made with love,
Salad days of blindness, secret saw the bloom.

Wherever we alone, no staring eyes, it was hot,
Youth reduced away like stock in boiling pot,
Nothing to burn, slowly the wild fire saw its end,
Out of its shell, from heat, the secret did creep.

Wet and slipped, puddles of emotionless tears,
Puddles to a stream, words poured heavy,
Glass dreams, iron plans, all washed away,
Water drained down, secret left on the ground.

His hidden root, her opened branches, stayed,
He, a cactus, she grew up to be a water lilly,
Dreams and secret on the soil, far from reach,
She looked up, he down, null and empty.

○

Of the burning crown

Concealed meaning birthed innocent laughs,
All ever wanted, his head under the crown,
Jokes at morn, treasonous plans, he coughed,
A devil about to prowl, masqueraded, a clown.

Concealed words inside innocent flattery,
Forced into a room, forged into a secret,
Befuddled into praise, tottered to butchery,
Nine months he waited, joking in discreet.

Concealed in white, under stranger's breast,
The baby was chased, the baby was raised,
Secret unfolded the treachery, a letter,
Written in blood, stamped by dying breath.

Concealed under the sun, in black he cloaked,
Jester among whores and wine, did drown,
Wish again true, head, now under a burning crown,
Dried bones and ash, in blood, left to soak.

○

The ravens spoke

One to another, black to white, the ravens spoke,
Was it ever serious or an end of the day joke?
A courier, secrets weighed more than a yoke,
Only saw tears, some peace to war, it stoke.

Easy for you, holding the power of color,
Ours too, along with yours brought privilege,
Ours, pay for every breath, a hefty demurrage,
Your secrets were good, mine always a squalor,
Mine was threats, pleadings and forced parley.

Was shot down, the beholder disliked the tone,
Burned, when the revealed secrets spoke freedom,
It it's a community, we both are loathed alike,
Poked belief, even secrets wished it wasn't alive,
World's changing, their views evolve seldom,
Hatred spry, even what remains, is just your bone.

○

Precious Red

Every First breath accompanies the loss of blood,
Only time in life a mother smiled, When we cried,
A beginning covered in red, till the end they bled,
Amidst all this , for peace and joy they always vied.

An age comes, cycle starts, and again they've to shed,
Monthly period of pain, few days of altering mood,
Stain of that red, something that is still being mocked,
Inept to that pain, over silly things we men just brood.

To fulfill lust, soulless bodies prey on them and feed,
Again that red shed, a place in the society gets denied,
Punish the victim with hatred became everyone's creed,
In suicide or solitude, their life gets deeply buried.

To love or not, still determined by the same bloodshed,
Character of a woman concluded by that same bloodshed,
War, murder or sacrifice, all ends in bloodshed,
But, for a woman, that remains their precious red.

○

A letter from Silence

Years passed, many to come, these words I say,
Were served before, struggles had them eaten,
Time will sway, will be hot as in the month of May,
Always remember, I have ears and I will listen.

Tongues like swords, your defeat they wrest,
Eyes with blatant lies, set to put you in a trap,
War, you hate, peace like a slave, they molest,
Patience, a virtue, my wisdom will guide like a map.

Arduous life among hypocrites, many, a ponce,
Plethora of selfishness, impel the quiet to bend,
Mocking quietitude, unknown to it's power to upend,
I am calm before the storm, this I enounce.

All born in silence, most chose to roar like thunder,
Cull to the society, still you stayed with me in mirth,
Will lead in this world, a life on an outlander,
But, I will bless, till they all know your worth.

○

Wild flower

Ever wondered what exactly is the meaning of wild?
I found out,it's something difficult for one to accept,
Blind to the real beauty, I took the flower and began to gild,
Later, eyes opened and I looked back, those petals wept,
It asked me for a reason, gave a hurtful and cruel answer,
That you're disparate, a flower that grew in the wild.

All it expected was to be blessed, a spring that's mild,
To be loved and remembered, once dead, body to be kept,
Among the pages of my heart, cherished like an innocent child,
Dreams can be wild, but in reality, I failed to accept,
Lived among the harsh world, into hands of Earth it wither,
The one that always grew under the shade, my wild flower.

○

A Mystique Rover

They say he rides on human spirits as horses,
many mysteries to unravel,
He lives long enough like those unending roads
one possibly could travel,
Feeding on your fear and moxie, upon every
hidden desire he revel,
He dwells on a floating tree, every leaf engraved
his journey as a novel,
Survival of his home on the balance between good
and bad, or it shrivel,
Depth of its roots inside every virtuous and evil brains,
one could only marvel.

Some say he's an enormous beast, some, he resembles
a group of pixies,
Few believes he is a she, a small group proclaims him
a collection of fantasies,
Everything opposite, day is night, night a day, in his
mystical forest of ecstasy,
Many wanders in search, only to be revealed when
you rise up in apostasy,
Or else, flies uncaptured through generations,
like a prophecy,
Riding on human spirits from birth to death, and after,
amidst their hypocrisy.

○

Stone and Flesh

A decision to be made, the secret was told,
The one, none alive nor dead ever knew,
The hell frightened him less than the one,
Now he roams, whom to blame for the one?

Tame the secret, bound it to love's chains,
Deepest dungeon, known to one, unknown to few,
Days were young, when one chain rusted away,
Love was strong, when it shattered to pieces,
Void emotions, when it vanished into thin air,
Lust burned like sun, when it melted into nothing,
Peek into dungeon, secret was revealed, when,
It grew the chain, to a distance he couldn't behold.

It wasn't just the secret, it always had a rival,
And their everlasting war – the heart and the secret,
How it changed hin – half stone, half flesh,
Some saw only the stone, threw some on it,
The flesh is rock, decided some, and ran afar,
Out of fear, turned his back, back to the stone,
To anyone who wished to feel the flesh.

Now he roams, flesh covered in a stony cloak,
All around the world, whom to blame for the one?
Blame it on the stars, or the unaccepting society?
Blame it on its blood or the mind that thinks?

A decision to be made, the secret was told,
The one,None alive nor the dead ever knew,
The hell frightened him less than the one,
Now he roams, whom to blame for the one?

○

Handle "CARE" with care

I doubted myself a million times,
Brutally killed myself plenty of times,
Here I stand, convicted of those heinous crimes,
Staring at the plain sky, my life is a mime.

Failed to understand those fair appreciation,
Now, surrounded by harsh voices of denunciation,
Were few, who loved and cared with elation,
Closed my senses at them, I'm watching my cremation.

Was blessed with two precious gifts from heaven,
Both made my sordid life a beautiful haven,
Today I broke one, balance of life uneven,
Peace, comfort. Shelter, lying down like fabric unwoven.

Whom to blame, my confused heart or inept brain?,
Days will be dull, nights will drown in disdain,
Body in shivers as if my hands had bloodstain,
Is it recoverable? Will I get it back?, I'm in pain,
All because I miserably failed to maintain.

Staring at the plain sky, my life is a mime.
Staring at the plain sky, my life is a mime.

○

Around us

Never expect anything in return, except,
Some love, nothing else, now a lost concept,
People wants something, better without a receipt,
Always in a rage, the growth of others they intercept.

Kindness these days are treated with disrespect,
Joy is found, everytime when its broken, a pact,
More the money is paid, more their pride erect,
Everytime it's forgotten, there's always an aftereffect.

Easy to see two bodies walking all the way together,
Known to the truth, their hearts are with some another,
Promises made to be with each other through any weather,
Let a sunny day come, their love, like flowers will wither.

This is the world we live in, all zealously jealous,
A mother dying in front of them, their hearts callous,
Unaware about the path being followed is perilous,
Time has shown, they all will die a death tremulous.

○

Bleeding red

Bite marks, nail scars, deed of an animal in human skin,
Covered in tar of mild lust, mercy thrown into a bin,
Plundering the peace and innocence by a deadly sin.

Darkness of the pain, light being lost, it bled red,
Bedsheet or raw earth, blindly covered them in red,
One fine day, to face it all, decided in agony, the red,
All, the silent white, pushed into the night the weak red,
Fell down, bled red, looked up, moon was blood red,
Only black to be seen, rest all, eyes shut, acted dead.

Is rape confined only to something that's sexual?
Can it be common for anything that's not mutual?
Mock her body, word-raping her sense of being equal,
Hardwork looked down, a daily rape that's accrual,
These are few, the numbers will grow, its eventual,
Physical or mental, rape in any form always bleed red.

○

Remorseless cadence

These days humans tread on foot, rumors on white horse,
Putting an end to those who believe in its course,
Around us, those who wish to see the real picture, sparse,
Hearts painted black, eyes blind to truth, days now worse,
Expired souls carried everyday on our bodies as hearse.

Getting killed is considered a blessing, being loved, a curse,
Innocent's plead music to ears, cry of a baby is hoarse,
Portrayal of fake sympathy common, empathy averse,
Greed on high gear will one day on permanent reverse,
Roads seem perfect, in the end, through hell they traverse.

Words that flow, deeds that follow, badly perverse,
Tearing blameless lives, the subject they converse,
Money, their God, greed and vendetta they disburse,
Profit and gain, in sinless blood they immerse,
Time will transpire, they be dealt by their own universe.

o

Gate Keeper

Under the white oak tree, dwelled a blind dwarf,
Half skull, half heart tattoo, hid behind a scarf,
Cursed, greed and goodness, he did snarf,
Dark emotions tied to his oak rod, like boats in a wharf.

Heart turns red whenever a good deed is done,
During a bad deed, a leaf from the tree will be gone,
Light had to lurk in evil, for every sin he had to atone,
Eat from the rod, from destruction, this world be condoned.

Was ruthless in his times, nature called him the "Ripper",
Mercilessly killed anything, even family, that he saw prosper,
On a thunderous night, the curse, nature did whisper,
The balance of good and evil – he is now a gate keeper.

○

Only look on mockery

Thousand questions under restless
hearts in an infuriated fray,
Hoping that the fight with destiny
turns out to be a fairplay,
Always probing into other's life,
their emotions we blindly slay,
In course of that hunt, some
shatters like a pot of clay.

An ordinary demise of a joyous man
invokes never a query,
But his unexpected demise, entails
the possibility of a mystery,
In a rummage for reasons, regrets
or hidden secrets so leery,
Portrayed joy, barring mouths
of close ones, mystery turns eerie.

One among many, when realized,
emotions are pretentious apery,
Smiles painted like clowns, death
reveals their concealed dupery,
Pestering other lives in horrifying
way, few on bustling venery,
Deceptive secrecy, unfolds nothing,
whether content or life so lowery.

Beholding life so perfect, in this world,
is just a common flattery,

 | Joseph Idicheria

Shadowing that gaudery, hides your vision
to a welcome so wintery,
Not to hurt others, is explainable
to cloak your misery,
Coming through all that without
ending life is real bravery.

○

An upstage view

Many are there, wanting others to
witness their drama on stage,
To be one, to take one under their
arms, a protégé,
Toil and moil their days off, to be
bellowed a great mage,
Realization they lack, already on one,
surrounded like a cage,
Memories, most of them, when reminisced,
made under a false image,
Trust and betrayal, silence and violence,
few among the wage.

Actors, the most famous, are ruthless
pretending to be a sage,
Most admire, the power to hide
under the skin, their ravage,
Few forced into many roles, to make
two ends meet in a forage,
Hope lost, success of villains, seen as
this world's visage,
Dreams of the hardworking, opportunities
of deserving, they pillage,
True meaning, purpose of life, a hoax for
them, to be thrown offstage.

People are wandering, burdened shoulders,
a better day as luggage,
For that one thing, to bring back those

old days, they rummage,
Considering all those villainous, an illusion
fading away like a mirage,
A day filled with goodness will stay a myth,
I presage,
An untiring will, a kind heart can break
from the long lasting bondage,
Many dreams to unfold, as they
set the sails for a hopeful voyage.

O

From underneath

Immix, my stance amidst birth and death,
Immane, the visions of reality and dream,
Immesh, are the shadows of past and future,
Immure, my body, secrets done and undone,
Immure to the tentacles of fate and destiny.

Deep underneath the soil, my soul immersed,
Hurled my help, now in need of miracle, immense,
Robbed my breath, stained hands of immoral,
Lie my festering debris, silent and immotile,
Yet, the secrets, their desires, it immolate.

Immanent was I, hiding evidences with clues,
Imminent, an eye behold, an ear hearken,
Day when sun's cold, moon dark, none immortal,
Ones who served, discard them like immigrants,
Immutable the secret and its advent in immediacy.

○

Clowns of Mockersdale

They were seven, and every evening
they tell a discrete tale,
People of that town, old to young, gathered
together with a glass of ale,
The stage over a graveyard named
"Mocker's Bed", in town of Mockersdale,
Those seven existed for generations,
imitating every headstone's telltale,
Onlooking all emotions alive and dead,
they, the Clowns of Mockersdale.

Survived many years unharmed by emotions,
their body and mind still hale,
All their tales left a painful mark
on people like that of a wale,
Color painted on their faces, varied with
every story's morale,
And those, were not of and for the dead,
where from the living's locale,
Motive, protect outside world from town's
heartless souls and tattertale.

The clowns chained those people
together in their stories bale,
They knew, if released, can transmute
real emotions to fake and stale,
These days, clowns in agony, hurt by stake
of dark emotions that impale,

If, for once, had to paint faces black,
it infers their life's finale,
With concealed tears, for the rest,
they carry on with their regale.

O

Affair to kill

Draped her, in her shiny red velvet,
Hung her under the sky, pink and set,
Walked towards black and empty night,
Left behind all the white and its fight.

In her memory, built a red brick wall,
Nailed all memories and my blue soul,
Slept a peaceful night, bed of yellow rose,
It did, yes, my grey dreams did froze.

Nothing scarier, a rumor turned fact,
Nothing lovelier, a promise made a pact,
Everything it takes, broken trust to mend,
Everything it takes, simple doubt to forfend.

Was in love for numerous years,
Blindness caved in, offered only tears,
Under the purple sky, love lost it's way,
Salt met brown earth, nothing yet to say.

Heat and moans, silver linen made wet,
Saw them both, many times, still I bet,
Weakness and dead brain, finally met,
He left her to regret and as my target.

Draped her, in her shiny red velvet,
Hung her under the sun, pink and set,
Prick from yellow's thorn, I made to see,
Wasn't him, before and then. Was only me.

○

Inside the well of dead humanity

Never ever I knew, few scars can keep
out of sight my identity,
From one scary night till this, at war
between memories and reality,
Now, my body, a means for venery,
broken pieces hurling in pain's asperity,
Dollar bills gleaming under moonlight,
a new face welcomed with forceful alacrity,
Tried to find some emotions other
than lust, he offered scarcity,
That night I knew, few scars can
conceal anyones's identity.

Life was good, both happy, days blessed
with graceful felicity,
Every evening, picked from work,
rode behind, all over the busy city,
Waking up to smell of coffee, dozing off
on his scent, inexplicable serenity,
Only us, on the rocks on a beach,
one moment fell with some atrocity,
He laid unconscious, me raped heartlessly
with pure malignity.

Few days later, woke up to smell of smoke,
dim lights, unseen part of the city,
Stood in agony, stared at a broken mirror,
scars of fate's cruelty,
Drugged, couldn't resist or escape,
but endure the torture in continuity,

Every time the door opened, got offered
with food to survive the scurrility,
Any resistance, embellished my body,
new scar with animosity.

Searched for his face among many,
joy to be found will be aplenty,
That new face, the one who raped me,
fell into the pit of unstability,
Held myself together, to find out the face
I searched, waiting for his turn in amenity,
All the darkness I suffered for nothing,
but for wait of death's penalty,
That day I knew, even one scar can,
from love, seal your identity.

The love I had for him, caught me
off-guard, a moment of vulnerability,
Unrecognizable, the scars made me,
tears of my existence's clandestinity,
He kissed me, lingered on my bosom,
heart behind the dark unfamiliarity,
That, burned my little hope left in me,
the fire of fate's inexorability,
I laid still till he finished, open for
everyone my body till eternity,
Under the scar by his money,
I buried forever my lost identity.

○

Thrown in a bottle

A weird dream I had, in recent nights,
He confined, a transparent aura around,
He did float, he did sail, as if he knew
Where hope rises and sets inside me.

Aura, black and white under serene night,
Half blue and half orange at dawn,
Blinding white, I can't see, in afternoon,
Reddish pink, when the mighty sun sets.

With feet bonding sand and the sea,
Three days gone, since the dreams I had seen,
Kneeled on my knees, to hold a shell,
Graced my hand, a clean and dirty glass bottle.

It didn't break or end up in a belly,
Didn't sink or beheld someone's eyes,
What if it held his last breath?, or,
His last message, dead or alive?
Eager to read, hated to open,
Hanged in my room, under sun and moon,
Will read before I die, hopefully soon.

○

Two keys and a door

Deaden by the closed door ahead,
Fuddled, sips from demented mead
Of life, from within, choices to knead,
Whisper beyond, "love or freedom"?
Held the keys, decisions right, seldom,
Two keys unalike, opens that one door,
To a tumultuous sea or silent arbor,
Inept, chose one and ran, and forgot.

Woke to cold and murk, the sun gone,
That shone always, never set on me,
Fear crept in, murmur of breaking bone,
Nothing to feel, blackness only, to see,
Reason behind, that one choice I made.

Decide, to bail out or just sit and wail,
One sound, a scent gave their trail,
Through mud and stones, arms flail,
Felt like in a box, confined to a jail,
Pain and grief, the body lied senseless.

Raindrop trickled down the dried cheek,
Eyes beheld above, a rainbow in beam,
Retreating blackness, light over the dark,
To hold up, appeared, little baby stars,
The dark ahead, I see, but, this just a start,
The ones above, shines the path they chart,

The whisper of every rain, like Mozart,
Blackness lies, just a color in life's art,
That Whisper beyond, "Do you know?"
Teary eyes, "I do, I chose freedom".

○

To all those...

To all those single amidst many couples,
To all who love silence, trying to be empathetic,
To all who move back when the word fails you,
Let me tell you, I also do understand.

To all those who pushes people away,
To all those who crumble in a relation,
To all who believe they're not worth to be loved,
Let me tell you with assurance, I understand.

To all those in endless search of love,
To all who fail to understand and share love,
To all who fail to give and make love,
Let me tell you with a promise, you're not alone.

To all those failing to find love behind our silence,
To all who has no patience to see our love bloom,
To the world, I proclaim, still we will smile,
There's a world we dwell imagining feeling loved.

O

Aging Days

I was in a different world, filled with
tenderness and warmth,
It was the first day of my life,
life was simple and eath,
Nothing lasts forever, in a new world,
had to take my first breath,
In the beginning I was alone,
in latter surrounded by many kith,
From first step to last word,
everything was of great pith,
Moments set off to be experiences,
to memories in many ways,
Revelation of mortality, along the journey
in a world of aging days.

Times saw me going under so deep
among emotions in routh,
Got saved by those experiences
and little bit of faith,
Enacted many roles from birth till
end of my youth,
Very few, very lucky to reminisce
those gone days with mirth,
Purpose fulfilled or not, have to
wait for eminent death,
Once had memories, today, I'm a memory,
under a wreath,
Revelation of mortality, end of journey
through world of aging days.

○

 | Joseph Idicheria

The Grave Gossips

It was hell with her, such a condescending woman,
Thank god for eternity of peace in the new domain.

That one's a hypocrite, bawled against body shaming,
Look at her now, all skinny and scarily scrawny,
Don't be so naïve, it wasn't her choice, even for us.

I hate him very much, cheated on me outside these gates,
Now, sleeping next to another in front of my eyes.

He was always a show-off, never slept without his bling,
Bed from costly wood with his gold, to lie like a king.

A line to sum up life, name and age on a stone,
Everything has a story to be told, even the dry bones.

A fantasy – why should only living have fun,
When the dead can shoot gossip like bullets from gun.

o

An affair called life

You know when its about to drizzle,
Clouds declare with a loud whistle,
First drop caress the soul of the soil,
Outpour of the hoard, brim of the spoils,
Then, and then only, my ash you cast,
Hark back only the beaut, of my past,
Let some coalesce, soar with petrichor,
Rest, with the wind, the world it explore.

Treaded, learned, in the erroneous road,
Drowned, bathed in the memory's sea,
Felt, hurt, burnt, unwilted in life's fire,
Meditated, levitated, in essence of space,
This, story of some breaths in the earth.

Tis, last words mine to you, your future,
You won't see me, ever and that's for sure,
Conceived in pain, perceived your effort,
Master it, emotions in our hands, a puppet,
Shatter your heart twice, then sing a duet,
With one besides you, even if its an escort,
Every rise of moon, consider an end,
Acknowledge what I've bequeathed,
Every sunset, always a beginning,
At all times, there lies a new winning,
Revel, in the permanence of temporary,
Until you're invited to forever slumbery,
Tis, last words of mine to you, your future,
You won't see me, ever and that's for sure.

○